D0114509

# When Leadership and Discipleship Collide

Also by Bill Hybels

*Holy Discontent*

*Just Walk Across the Room*

*The Volunteer Revolution*

*Courageous Leadership*

*Rediscovering Church* (with Lynne Hybels)

*Honest to God?*

*Fit to Be Tied* (with Lynne Hybels)

*Descending Into Greatness* (with Rob Wilkins)

*Becoming a Contagious Christian* (with Mark Mittelberg and Lee Strobel)

# WHEN
# LEADERSHIP
# AND DISCIPLESHIP
# COLLIDE

## BILL
## HYBELS

ZONDERVAN®

WILLOW
Willow Creek Resources

ZONDERVAN.com/
AUTHORTRACKER
follow your favorite authors

*When Leadership and Discipleship Collide*
Copyright © 2007 by Bill Hybels

Requests for information should be addressed to:
Zondervan, *Grand Rapids, Michigan 49530*

---

Library of Congress Cataloging-in-Publication Data

Hybels, Bill.
    When leadership and discipleship collide / Bill Hybels.
        p. cm. — (Leadership library)
    ISBN-13: 978-0-310-28306-5
    ISBN-10: 0-310-28306-X
    1. Bible. N.T. Mark—Criticism, interpretation, etc. 2. Leadership—Biblical teaching.
    3. Christian leadership. 4. Leadership—Religious aspects—Christianity. I. Title.
    BS2585.6.L42H93 2007
    253—dc22                                                          2007012728

---

This edition printed on acid-free paper.

*Interior design by CHANGE Design Group*

*Printed in the United States of America*

---

07 08 09 10 11 12 13 • 10 9 8 7 6 5 4 3 2 1

# LEADERSHIP LIBRARY

The purpose of the Leadership Library is to provide leaders in all arenas—churches, businesses, schools, or nonprofits—with the cutting-edge thinking and the practical advice they need to take their leadership skills to the next level.

Books in the Leadership Library reflect the wisdom and experience of proven leaders who offer big insights in a pocket-size package. Whether you read these books on your own or with a group of colleagues, the Leadership Library presents critical insight into today's leadership challenges.

# When Leadership and Discipleship Collide

**H**ands down, the single most impressive leader in the history of the world is Jesus of Nazareth. Now, I don't say that just because I'm a card-carrying Christian, which I am, but because I believe the facts speak for themselves. No leader ever cast a more expansive or breathtaking vision—nothing less than the redemption of the planet—than did Jesus Christ. No leader ever built a higher-impact team in a shorter period of time with less talent to work with. No leader ever instilled deeper values or inspired people more than Jesus Christ—in many cases, enough for them to die for the cause. Certainly, no leader has ever changed the course of human history the way Jesus did . . . and is still doing, more than two thousand years later.

I'd say it all adds up to some pretty compelling leadership evidence: He was the best leader ever.

# Breaking Leadership Laws

Imagine my surprise recently when I decided to read through the New Testament book of Mark and noticed several occasions when Jesus seems willfully to violate well-known, widely accepted laws of leadership. My observations were more than a little shocking.

## Build a Team of Highly Qualified Leaders

The first place I noticed the greatest leader in human history breaking a fundamental law of leadership is in the very first chapter of Mark. Jesus has just lost his strongest ally, John the Baptist, who has been thrown in prison for taking the leaders of the day to task on their sinful behavior. John may have had some odd culinary preferences and rather minimalist taste in attire, but you can't ask for a better ministry partner. He is bold, fearless, and fully devoted to the cause. Losing John to a jail cell is a huge hit to Jesus, and the pressing question on his mind must be, Who in the world do I recruit to replace a superstar like John?

Jesus is a religion teacher, so how about adding a rabbi to the ranks? Or a highly trained Pharisee, maybe, or a well-respected Sadducee? What about some brilliant students of the Torah, a few leader types who are well schooled in Jewish custom?

No, Jesus goes out and instead gathers a rather motley crew of commercial fishermen. The majority of them are untrained, uncouth, and underage. Some have hot tempers, others have questionable business practices, and not one has evangelistic experience.

Imagine my surprise recently when I decided to read through the New Testament book of Mark and noticed several occasions when Jesus seems willfully to violate well-known, widely accepted laws of leadership.

It is a leadership violation to beat all leadership violations, but despite everyone's raised eyebrows, Jesus plows ahead, confident he has made the right decision.

## Keep Up the Momentum

The next place I noticed Jesus breaking a law of leadership is found later in the first chapter of Mark. Jesus' popularity is building. The crowds are getting larger everywhere he goes. People see Jesus driving out evil spirits, healing sick people, preaching the kingdom of God, and they wonder if he might actually be the long-awaited Messiah. Right in the middle of this "Nielsen-rating" upswing, Mark 1:35 records that Jesus actually *withdraws* from all the action; he goes off alone to a solitary place to reflect and spend some quality time in prayer.

Obviously, this is in clear violation of the well-known law of momentum. Every leader knows how hard it is to establish momentum. And every leader knows that once you get it established, you should do whatever it takes to keep it going. Momentum is one of a leader's closest allies. When the energy's high and the team is strong and people are buzzing, the last thing you want to do is pull the momentum plug.

But Jesus walks away from it all, a decision that really miffs his disciples, who are still flying high on the buzz of effective ministry. They quickly pull together a search party and, upon finding their fearless leader, reprimand him for leaving, "Jesus, everyone is looking for you!" Which is simply code for: "What's up with this? We've all been busting our backsides to get this kingdom dream realized for you, and now that we're on a roll, you want time off for a spiritual retreat?!"

From a leadership perspective, Jesus' seclusion makes zero sense, and the disciples know it. The greatest leader of all time violates a Leadership 101–level law, to the great shock of his followers . . . and me.

## Propagate Good Press

Soon afterward, a man with leprosy approaches Jesus and says, in Mark 1:40, "If you are willing, you can make me clean." A hush settles over the watching crowd. Ants stop. Birds stare. Angels lean forward from their seats in heaven. Everyone knows that this diseased man has lived a pitiable existence his entire life. Leprosy has left him disfigured, excluded, and, according to Jewish custom, ceremonially unclean. The one person on the planet who possesses the power and authority to take away his physical, mental, and emotional anguish, Jesus Christ, now stands just two feet from him. Talk about a media event in the making!

Jesus knows the guy is in a sorry state. He also knows that the man is about to be completely and instantaneously healed. Facing a pending miracle of this magnitude, any leader worth his salary and bonuses would summon his PR folks and sanction a full-scale press conference. Rally the reporters and get the cameras rolling! This one will blow viewers away!

A hush settles over the watching crowd. Ants stop. Birds stare. Angels lean forward from their seats in heaven.

Mark 1:41 says, "Jesus . . . reached out his hand and touched the man." As a result, the man's leprosy departs from his body. But instead of trumpeting his success on the evening news, he looks at the leprosy-free man and says, in verse 44, "See that you don't tell this to anyone."

Surely it was just a lapse in leadership judgment on Jesus' part. I mean, if you're trying to magnetize people to your mission, the last thing you want to do is *squelch* good press!

## Avoid Unnecessary Controversy

Every leader knows that it's impossible to please all the people all the time; it's one of those leadership truths that just comes with the territory. But seasoned leaders also understand that stirring up *unnecessary* controversy should be avoided at all costs. In other words, if you're going to receive some kicking and screaming as a result of a hard decision, then at least be sure it's the right decision, made at the right time. Why spend credibility capital if you don't have to?

A pastor called me a while back. He was from a very conservative church that was right in the middle of its largest capital campaign ever. One of the elders wanted to open up a discussion about changing the anti-alcohol policy that the church had upheld proudly for a hundred years. The pastor was inclined to agree with this elder and asked for my opinion on the matter. I answered him in two words: "Not now!"

Then to clarify, I said, "Take my word for it: you must be *very* careful not to stir up unnecessary conflict during critical eras of church building. Open up that issue for discussion at some point, maybe, but *don't* do it now."

When I read the second chapter of the Gospel of Mark, however, I found an instance where Jesus completely disregards this law of avoiding unnecessary controversy.

By way of context, Jesus has just completed several miraculous healings, including the now-famous one where a paralytic man is lowered through a hole in the roof into a meeting room where Jesus is speaking. The man wants to be healed, and nothing is going to stop him from landing in the presence of the One who can heal him.

As a result of all this fanfare, the crowds surrounding Jesus and his followers are building once more, and townspeople are all brimming with energy about Jesus' miraculous ministry. Momentum is on Jesus' side again, and everything seems to be heading up and to the right.

It was not the brightest of leadership decisions, you might say . . . at least on the surface. All things considered, would twenty-four hours really have made *that* big a difference?

Until one day—a Sabbath, mind you—when Jesus decides to get some fresh air with his disciples. They wind up walking through some guy's grain field, and the disciples start popping the heads off several stalks to snack on. The Pharisees, who never seem to be far from the action, absolutely go nuts and consider the grain-popping motion an act of labor, which is strictly forbidden by their rules. If Jesus allows this sort of reaping on the Sabbath, they think, who *knows* what's next?

Jesus explains the whole bit about the Sabbath being created for people, not the other way around, but the

Pharisees aren't easily dissuaded. They turn on their heels and head off to set their next trap for Jesus. Before long, they will lure him into committing yet another Sabbath infraction and as a result have him turned over to the Herodians, the group which will ultimately plot his horrific death.

Talk about having stirred up a hornet's nest of controversy! Really now, couldn't he have waited until *Monday* to take the disciples on their little joy walk?

It was not the brightest of leadership decisions, you might say . . . at least on the surface. All things considered, would twenty-four hours really have made *that* big a difference?

## Leverage Time and Influence

As if all of the preceding violations aren't enough, Jesus makes another colossal leadership blunder in Mark 10, when he breaks the law of wisely leveraging time and influence. Every leader knows that you only have so many hours in a day; to be effective, you must figure out which people will move the mission ahead the most and then spend time with those people. The rest of the folks are going to have to find their own way. You have a job to do, and to do it well, you have to leverage your influence with the people who can make things happen. Again, this is one of those no-brainer fundamentals of leadership.

In verse 13, Jesus is caught spending time in the middle of a workday with a group of children. Surely there are more important things he can be doing: preparing sermons, leadership development, strategic planning, whatever. Blowing his afternoon on a bunch of pesky half-pints makes no leadership sense. The disciples are all too aware of this, so they decide to take matters into their own hands. They tell the kids, as well as the parents of the kids, to get lost: Don't they know that Jesus has very important things to do, people to see, places to go?

Jesus is a little less than thrilled by the disciples' interference. He severely rebukes them for pushing the children away and, in essence, says, "I alone will decide who is worth my time and energy, whether you guys agree with me or not. If I want to hang out with kids, it's my prerogative, no matter what leadership law gets violated."

## Don't Bite the Hand that Feeds You

How about another one? Shortly after that occasion, Jesus thoroughly alienates a very wealthy man. Remember his interaction with the rich young man? This breaks a cardinal rule pertaining to fundraising: Don't make wealthy people mad! You'll probably need their help sooner or later, so don't offend them without good reason. But Jesus goes right for this rich man's jugular, spiritually speaking. And sure enough, Mark 10:22 reveals that this

> Jesus thoroughly alienates a very wealthy man ... This breaks a cardinal rule pertaining to fundraising: Don't make wealthy people mad!

first-century investment-banker-type heads off, having made *no* contribution to Jesus' cause. You tell me: was that wise leadership on Jesus' part?

Still want more?

## Avoid Sensational Exploits

In Mark 11, Jesus cleanses the temple of money changers and marketers who are peddling their wares in a house of worship. (It actually *needed* a good cleansing, but that's beside the point.) Jesus' motivation may be pure, but any student of leadership has to wonder if the whip (John 2:15) is really all that necessary. All the whip is going to do is give the press something to sensationalize, and seasoned leaders never give free bullets to the opposition. If he has to turn over a few tables, fine, the point has to be made. But lose the whip. Where's the common sense there?

## Demonstrate Unshakeable Courage

Perhaps the most extreme example of Jesus breaking a leadership law occurs just before his betrayal and arrest in the Garden of Gethsemane. In Mark 14 we find the city of Jerusalem in an uproar. There are vicious rumors floating around that someone will be paid to kill Jesus and his disciples. The emotional climate is intense.

So, to counterbalance the fear his followers are feeling, what does a veteran leader like Jesus Christ do? One might think he would demonstrate unshakeable courage and then call his followers up to his level of steadfastness, a la William Wallace in the movie *Braveheart*. When his soldiers were thinking about defecting from an impending major battle, Wallace (played masterfully by Mel Gibson) mounts his horse and rides back and forth in front of all the soldiers, shouting, "I am not afraid to die for our cause on this day, and you shouldn't be either!"

Talk about inspiring! After seeing that scene, even I was ready to sign up for action. Which is huge, given the fact that I am a notorious chicken when it comes to fighting and hate violence of any kind.

With fear-stricken disciples huddled around him in the Garden of Gethsemane, Mark 14:34 reveals an extremely distressed, deeply troubled Jesus: "My soul is overwhelmed with sorrow," he admits, even "to the point of death." Jesus asks three of his men to join him in prayer—a heartfelt prayer in which he asks his heavenly Father if the mission that was assigned to him could please be amended or taken away. To paraphrase, he says, "Take this cup from me if at all possible, Father. But, if not, then your will be done."

It's a far cry from *Braveheart*.

And a far cry from any sort of adherence to the leadership laws I know. The laws I know dictate that leaders must never show personal vulnerability in the midst of a mission-threatening crisis. Being wobbly and weepy when the stakes are high . . . is that really the best way to serve the team and the cause?

Now, to be clear, despite Jesus' moment of fear, he quickly finds the courage to get up, endure horrendous

> B
> Being wobbly
> and weepy when the stakes
> are high . . . is that really
> the best way to serve
> the team and
> the cause?

suffering, and voluntarily lay down his life for sin-scarred people like you and me. He does precisely what he has come to earth to do. He completes his redemptive mission. But that momentary transparency into his emotional struggle—the display of weakness and uncertainty in the Garden—makes me wonder what this leader was thinking!

# Leadership Violations Committed by Yours Truly

I read through the entire book of Mark, noting these very interesting situations where Jesus seems to violate long-held laws of leadership, and, to be perfectly honest, it was a bit unsettling. I began to wonder: *Have I ever, throughout the course of my thirty-plus years in leadership, knowingly broken the laws of leadership?*

To my surprise, nearly half a dozen violations came to mind.

I began to wonder: *Have I ever, throughout the course of my thirty-plus years in leadership, knowingly broken the laws of leadership?*

## Bet on a Ragtag Team

The very first law I broke was when I decided who would be on the church-planting team that would establish Willow Creek Community Church. Every leader knows how important it is to surround yourself with the highest caliber people you can find: the brightest, most capable, most competent ones available. But for some strange reason, I took a completely different course of action when God prompted me to start Willow. Instead of recruiting high-capacity types, I surrounded myself with a few personal friends, none of whom had any specific experience, expertise, or talent in church work.

One friend was fresh out of the military and trying very hard to get off a bad marijuana habit. Another was just back from South America, where his missionary parents had dragged him along. To say he was spiritually disillusioned would be a gross understatement: he didn't have much use for God, he didn't go to church, and he was intolerant of anything that smacked of religiosity. Another was a high school buddy who had dropped out of college because he had no clue what he wanted to do with his life.

These guys were no *Who's Who* in church planting.

The leader in me knew that I was signing up for all sorts of unnecessary risk with this ragtag group, but whenever I prayed about who was supposed to help me start Willow, the Spirit would whisper the same three names over and over again: *Tim, Scott, and Joel.* So that's who I chose. Thirty-one years later, these guys are still with me; it can accurately be said that Willow Creek Community Church was built on their shoulders as much as mine.

Of course, I would never advise a young church planter or a business entrepreneur to assume this measure of senseless risk when launching a brand-new endeavor; I'd never suggest putting such fragile eggs in the basket of an inexperienced ad hoc group of non-leaders. But that's exactly what I did. I knew I was headed down a path that seemed to violate a critical leadership law, but I also knew that God was the one leading. And so I followed.

## Derail the Momentum Train

When I read the occasion in the first chapter of Mark where Jesus seemingly disregards the law of momentum, a memory from my own leadership journey sprang to mind. In the late eighties, Willow was growing by hundreds of people a month, and reporters began to write articles about "this ministry in Chicago" that was rapidly becoming the largest church in North America. Despite the positive attention, I had the sickening feeling that even though people were filling up our auditorium, they weren't necessarily becoming fully devoted followers of Christ. This was a problem for one simple reason: our mission was (and still is, actually) to turn irreligious people into fully devoted followers of Christ.

We were building a crowd, but we weren't building committed followers. We weren't facilitating the type of growth that would one day birth an "Acts 2 church"—a people marked by their acceptance of seekers, their devotion to Scripture and prayer, their generosity with material possessions, their consistency of fellowship, and so forth.

> I made my
> toughest ministry
> decision to date: I
> intentionally derailed
> our momentum.

I spent some time with God hashing through this
dilemma. I rallied some of my most trusted friends and
advisers and, after factoring in their assessments and
advice, I made my toughest ministry decision to date:
I intentionally derailed our momentum. I interrupted
whatever was on the preaching docket to do a six-week
series about the cost of following Christ, including
no-holds-barred teaching about the requirements of
discipleship. I wanted our entire congregation to understand
what "full commitment to Jesus Christ" really meant. It was

during this time that I coined the expression: "Ninety-five percent commitment to Christ is 5 percent short."

I asked every person in the auditorium why on earth they would consider giving less than their *absolute* best to the One who had given his best for them. I beat that drum for six weeks straight.

This approach certainly flattened out our growth curve. Worse than that reality, though, was the nagging realization that I'd developed a split personality. The leadership side of me screamed, *You're an idiot! You wrecked the church's momentum!* while another voice whispered, *Way to go, Bill! You're doing exactly what I want you to do. You're not just building a crowd; you're building fully devoted followers of Jesus Christ. You're really trying to establish an Acts 2 church here, which is exactly what I called you to do. Way to go!*

The law of leadership fought tooth and nail to maintain momentum. But the quiet voice of the Holy Spirit told me something entirely different. This wouldn't be the last time the dichotomy occurred.

## Embrace Muslims after 9/11

I have a fairly high risk tolerance, so there are numerous examples of my stirring up unnecessary controversy. In this regard, I relate to Jesus' lawbreaking tendencies quite well. One instance in particular came to mind as I sat with pen in hand after my read-through of the Gospel of Mark. It had to do with a decision I made on the heels of 9/11.

Three or four months into our nation's healing following the terrorist attacks, things were still quite difficult for Muslims. In Chicago, for example, people were beaten on the street just because they were adherents of Islam; mosques were firebombed; death threats were made . . . all because of the backlash of 9/11. It was a senseless, heartless response to an already dreadful situation, and I felt that our church should do its part to put an end to the insanity.

I invited a local Muslim leader to attend our weekend services as a resource for greater understanding. I wanted to do a fifteen-minute interview about the true teachings of Islam and felt whatever risk I assumed was well worth it if it meant helping Willow's congregation grasp what the Koran really teaches about infidels, jihads, holy wars, violence, revenge, and other oft-misunderstood issues.

The goal, I kept reminding myself, was to build bridges by fostering acceptance and expanding perspectives. But that's not how things went down.

A conservative Christian magazine caught wind of the interview and proceeded to distort the facts in what can only be characterized as a nationwide, months-long *creaming*.

Interestingly, most people at Willow thought the service was extremely beneficial, that it did indeed serve as a bridge builder in our community. But I had risked a fair amount of national credibility capital and created "unnecessary controversy" on that one.

## Spend Time with Sam

Jesus seemingly violated the law of wisely leveraging time and influence when he blew an entire afternoon on a posse of kids. This is another law-breaking experience I can relate to.

Years ago, Willow engaged in an arduous effort to address an eighteen-million-dollar shortfall in our capital campaign. Other senior leaders and I were in the middle of conducting dozens of "vision tours," where I would lead hard-hat-clad Creekers through the parts of the new facility that were under construction and cast vision for the ministry that would take place there, once everything was funded. In addition, I wrote letters inviting people to give their best gifts—time, talents, treasures—to this effort. I met one-on-one with scores of donors and asked if they would pray about how they might help us.

Every moment of every day mattered—a lot!—during that era. But one afternoon, I did something that would have sounded the alarm bells in even the most novice leaders.

I answered my ringing cell phone to discover a man named Sam on the other end. Sam lives in South Haven, Michigan, where my family spends part of our summers. My wife, Lynne, and I had helped Sam buy a car wash one year so that he could keep his family from falling into a state of total financial ruin. Over a crackly connection that afternoon, Sam said he needed my help.

It took me two and a half hours to drive from Willow's campus in South Barrington to the car wash in South Haven, which is a long time to question the wisdom of taking such a trip. I arrived, greeted Sam, and took my seat across from him on an overturned five-gallon bucket in one of the wash bays. Pretty casual accommodations for a staff meeting, I thought, but I had bigger concerns on my mind, like, for starters, what on earth am I doing here when Willow obviously is destined for disaster?

Sam proceeded to tell me that he was a hundred and eighty dollars short that month. Personally, he didn't know how he was going to pay the rent and the electric bill, not to mention feed his family.

He began to describe his regrettable state of affairs to me, but I found myself struggling to pay attention. My mind was spinning a little regret-fueled tale of its own: *I can't believe you wound up here. You're some kind of leader, Bill, dropping everything, getting into your car, and lugging yourself all the way to Michigan, believing that somehow, someway, your random act of kindness would make a difference. Look at you, sitting here on a bucket, messing with Sam's hundred-and-eighty-dollar problem, when you should be leveraging your time with people who can help with the EIGHTEEN-MILLION-DOLLAR predicament you're in back home!*

That day, sitting with Sam on those overturned buckets in the car wash, I felt a *collision* of sorts, different from anything I'd ever known in my life. The leadership side of me was saying: *Get back to Barrington, Bozo! This is no time for charity; this is no time for sentimentality; this is no time for your heart to bleed for the condition of the poor. You can solve that when the campaign is over, but for now, get your rear in gear and get home!*

At the same time, another voice whispered: *I am so proud of you, Bill. Hang in there with Sam; dollar figures aside, his problem is just as big to him as yours is to you. I'm in this; I'll help you both meet the demands you face. For now, just be a friend to Sam.*

Jesus' words from Matthew 25:40 tipped the scales toward the voice vying for discipleship: "Whatever you did for one of the least of these brothers and sisters of mine, you did for me." As I drove away from the car wash that day, I sensed the whisper of the Spirit saying, *Bill, I'm working on you. Trust me, please. I'm working on you. Sam doesn't need your help as much as you think he does; rather, you *need what happens when you relate with him.*

I stayed the course with Sam until we could sort out his financial woes, and I will remember that meeting in the wash bay for a long, long time.

I wonder, do you know what that intersection collision between leadership and discipleship feels like? Have you established ahead of time which you will choose when the collision occurs? I remember well the first time I had to take my own medicine on this issue. It happened on a beautiful June morning, at a fishing derby, of all places.

## Prioritize the Fishing Derby

Special Friends is a ministry to more than fifty Willow families that have children with serious mental or physical challenges. Over the years, I have established some extraordinary friendships with some of these very brave young kids and their parents, but there's nothing necessarily rational about the soft spot in my heart I

Interestingly, though, the Spirit of God wasn't buying my excuses. He hounded me, chased me down, and just wouldn't let go.

have for them; as those who know me well can attest, the spiritual gift of mercy is noticeably absent in me. Still, whenever I can sneak into one of the Special Friends activities, I do.

One summer, our Special Friends ministry was holding its annual fishing derby at the lake on our campus and sent me a personalized invitation to attend. I gladly put it on my schedule, but then some travel complications made me doubt whether it would all work out. As the Saturday morning of the derby drew near, things weren't looking good. I tried to rationalize my way out of feeling guilty for missing the event. I listed five airtight reasons why a leader with my level of responsibility had no business having a fishing derby on his calendar and why such an event should be an easy one for me to miss with no qualms whatsoever.

Interestingly, though, the Spirit of God wasn't buying my excuses. He hounded me, chased me down, and just wouldn't let go. I'm not prone to hearing audibly from God, but honestly, it felt like the Spirit was saying to me in full voice: *Bill, if you get this decision wrong, if you can't fit this event into your carefully crafted, highly leveraged leadership schedule, you've lost the plot entirely. If you bow out of this event, I'm here to tell you, you are* seriously *screwed up!*

It began to feel like my presence with the Special Friends that day was a kind of pass/fail test for my inner person. I would soon learn that it was the focal point of a much deeper lesson God was trying to drill into me. I finally stopped rationalizing, justifying, and struggling about the whole deal; I changed a bunch of other plans and declared, once and for all, that I was going to the fishing derby.

I had a ball! I helped kids put worms on their hooks and toss their lines out into the lake, and I celebrated with each and every one of them as they caught fish. I did my very best to add to their joy and enthusiasm that bright, sunny day, but when I drove home from the campus after the event had come to a close, the Spirit sort of killed my sunshine: *It shouldn't have been that hard, Bill. It really shouldn't have required this much of a struggle to get you to show up.*

Questions from heaven started popping up like little thought balloons above my sunburned head: *What's happening to you, Bill? Why was that such a traumatic decision? You better slow down your pace. You better think this stuff through, because plenty of these kinds of decisions will come your way in the future. Maybe now would be a good time to sort out how you will respond. Maybe you need to figure out what happens when the laws of leadership and the demands of discipleship collide, because every once in a while, they will. Mark my words.*

Although the Spirit had given me a great book title, I was none too thrilled about the content: I knew I had a *ton* of work to do before I could provide answers to the issues he raised in my heart and mind on the trip home from the derby. I decided to commit every spare moment of discretionary thought time to this question: What will be my response when the laws of leadership and the demands of discipleship collide?

In the weeks and months to follow, I searched my soul, studied the Scriptures, talked to friends, and reviewed my leadership journey. Even now, I do not have it all figured out. But perhaps a few of my initial reflections will trigger thoughts and observations and opinions of your own as they pertain to this all-important question for every leader to answer.

# The Origin of the "Laws of Leadership"

The first task I undertook was to clarify what these "laws of leadership" really were and to ascertain where they originally came from. Author and leadership expert John Maxwell is a close personal friend, but when a guy like that puts out a book titled *The 21 Irrefutable Laws of Leadership*, and it sells millions of copies and helps leaders in every discipline around the world, doesn't it make you scratch your head a little? For me, some pretty interesting questions started surfacing. Like, are there really just

> Here's what I'm
> beginning to grasp: laws of
> leadership are really just
> descriptions of hard-learned lessons
> that, for hundreds of years, leaders
> have come to view as valuable
> guides toward mission
> achievement.

twenty-one leadership laws? What if there are nineteen?
Or twenty-eight? What if there are *two hundred and eighty-three* laws of leadership? Who chose twenty-one, anyway?
And who gets to decide how these laws get described?

Here's what I'm beginning to grasp: laws of
leadership are really just descriptions of hard-learned
lessons that, for hundreds of years, leaders have come
to view as valuable guides toward mission achievement.
Laws of leadership are, in essence, a collection of wisdom
principles, passed from one leadership generation to the
next. The principles can pertain to building profitable

> Leadership laws are not
> "inspired" by God in the same
> manner that we use the word
> *inspiration* when referring to Scripture.
> They are not inerrant, infallible,
> or immutable . . . but they are
> *extremely* valuable
> observations.

companies or championship athletic teams or fantastic, God-honoring ministries. They can be learned on the battlefield or in the boardroom, during training camp or a political campaign. The "laws" that emerge serve as boundary lines, in a sense, that denote the field of play. Step outside of them and leadership's penalty flags are likely to start flying.

That said, leadership laws are not "inspired" by God in the same manner that we use the word *inspiration* when referring to Scripture. They are not inerrant, infallible, or immutable in the way we understand those terms biblically, but they are *extremely* valuable observations that, when followed, can cause each successive generation of leaders to get better at leading whatever they're leading.

## When Leadership and Discipleship Dovetail

After nailing down my beliefs about the origin of leadership's laws, the first conclusion I came to regarding how to respond when discipleship demands intersect with those laws was this: I believe that, most of the time, the laws of leadership and the teachings of Scripture—particularly regarding embracing people living far from God and discipling those who have already made a faith decision—dovetail nicely. I think that collisions between leadership and discipleship are actually quite uncommon.

Jesus consistently manifested what we might consider traditional "leadership laws" throughout his ministry: he cast and consistently reinforced a God-given, crystal-clear vision. He was perpetually (annoyingly, even!)

"on purpose"; he poured into his team until the mission poured out of them; he resolved conflict immediately . . . with love *and* truth; the list could go on and on.

The violations—or apparent violations—that I referenced from the Gospel of Mark caught my attention because they were rare exceptions to Jesus' strong, steady, mostly predictable leadership patterns.

It has been my strong bias for the last thirty-plus years that Christian leaders must take full advantage of the accumulated teachings of every leadership generation that has gone before them. What we work for in ministry leadership is the single most important endeavor on planet Earth—the building of the kingdom of God. The potential of this kingdom is greater than any other, and the stakes involved in realizing it are higher. When we get it right, and especially when we don't, we impact people's *eternities.* It seems plain to me, then, that Christian leaders above all others would strive to be the most devoted, most faithful, most *astute* learners of leadership's laws.

In my opinion, good teaching will never be enough to build the kingdom of God. But combine good teaching with great leadership, and watch what God will do! I believe that theology and the laws of leadership can synergize beautifully, catalyzing growth at exponential rates in churches, ministries, and businesses. It's for this reason that I continue to challenge leaders: Read everything you can read about the laws of leadership. Go wherever leadership is taught. Get near leaders who are more advanced than you are. Keep growing. Keep challenging yourself! Keep getting better!

But there is more.

It seems plain to me, then, that Christian leaders above all others would strive to be the most devoted, most faithful, most *astute* learners of leadership's laws.

Shortly after the realization that leadership and discipleship rarely collide, a second conviction emerged as a result of my focused attention on the issue.

## Decide on the Side of Discipleship

In those rare cases when the human laws of leadership and the scriptural demands of discipleship *do* collide, decide on the side of discipleship every time. *Decide on the side of discipleship every* single *time.* Trust the promptings of the Holy Spirit, for they will help you at these deadly intersections.

When the demands of discipleship articulated in the Bible collide with human laws of leadership, read my lips: Defer to the Bible.

Much of the published leadership literature these days has come from secular leaders in secular arenas. While we can learn a lot from people in business and athletics and government and the military and so on, we cannot forget that, ultimately, Christians—in whatever arena they lead—are trying to build *God's* kingdom. From time to time, leadership lessons from the secular world do not translate well into the arena of kingdom building, and, as ministry leaders, we must remember that our operating values and our ultimate marching orders come from only one book—a book that is God breathed, Spirit inspired, perfect in its content, unchanging in its ability to transform lives.

When the demands of discipleship articulated in the Bible collide with human laws of leadership, read my lips: Defer to the Bible. Look to the Bible. Trust the Bible. And obey the Bible . . . *every* time.

Several years ago, I was asked to conduct an interview with an exceptionally bright, very capable young man who was being considered for a role on our staff. I was alerted by my colleagues, who had already met with this candidate, that he should pass the interview with flying colors. "He's fantastic! And we really need him," they explained. "Only ten minutes of your time is necessary for this one, Bill. Really, it's only a formality . . . we just need your final sign-off."

But five minutes into the interview, I felt trouble brewing in my spirit. I could see how smart and capable this person was, but I also saw a few red flags. In my opinion, he had an air of overconfidence that bordered on being prideful. I didn't want the interview to get ugly, but the Holy Spirit kept whispering: *Probe this, Bill. Push on it and see how he responds.*

So I pushed. And once again, his response was very alarming to me.

Despite this young man's obvious competence and talent, he was not at all open to my queries about pride. He refused to have a candid conversation about how he would behave in a structure of authority. He shut down when I tried to investigate his views on the differences between having independent strength versus contributing to the strength of a team. And from there, the interview became very difficult.

Now, the leadership laws would say: Look, he's a young buck with some rough edges, but the guy's potential is huge. Those rough edges will be ground off while he's making great gains for the organization, so just hire him.

The teachings of Scripture, however, are quite clear on pride and its implications. First Peter 5:5 says, "God opposes the proud but shows favor to the humble." Proverbs 16:18 notes, "Pride goes before destruction, a haughty spirit before a fall."

These verses and others flooded my mind. The whispers of the Spirit seemed to be shouting in my ear: *Take a pass on this guy. Leave the position open. Pray with the young man, wish him well, but don't you dare hire him.* No matter what the leader in me said to do, I knew I had to let this guy go elsewhere.

The candidate had terrific leadership potential, and I'm sure he could have catalyzed some very exciting activity around Willow Creek. But I couldn't disobey the Spirit by hiring him. At that interview, my understanding of Scripture collided with the laws of leadership, and I simply had to land on the side of discipleship. I slept well that night. I knew I had done the right thing.

Even in secular arenas, there will be times when you need to follow the demands of discipleship rather than the laws of leadership. Just because you lead in a secular context does not mean that you, as a believer, don't have the Spirit whispering wisdom into your mind and heart. At those times, friend, *listen*. And obey.

The interview experience I describe above has occurred numerous times for a COO of a large public company in the Midwest. A Christ-follower, he can't always explain to his nonbelieving CEO and board members why certain candidates who are stellar on paper don't pass muster with him. But after repeatedly ignoring the Spirit's whispers and suffering the consequences, he now views *every* key interview as a spiritual act of worship. "Guide me, God," he says quietly as he enters these situations. In his opinion, the Holy Spirit's enablement is the only way he can preserve his personal values, protect the integrity of his staff culture, and execute his leadership role with credibility. I wholeheartedly agree.

I know of a property manager in Michigan, a believer who had nearly half a million dollars extorted from him last year. The culprit was his personal finance associate, also a professing Christ-follower. Talk about a dicey situation: the property manager's attorney (not to mention his justice-seeking wife) advised him to consider a hefty lawsuit, but something in him wouldn't allow it. "I kept getting the feeling God was up to something bigger than restoring my bank account," he said.

He followed through on those promptings from the Spirit. In a move that stunned everyone involved, he refused legal action and committed himself to restoring the

This much I know:
you can't put a price tag on
being obedient to the Holy Spirit's
promptings. Even when you are the
only person who understands why
you are doing what you're doing,
walk confidently along the path
God paves for you.

decades-long friendship with his former finance associate.
He continues to trust God's promise of provision to cover
daily living expenses—expenses that never used to enter
his mind.

Sounds crazy, right? This much I know: you can't
put a price tag on being obedient to the Holy Spirit's
promptings. Even when you are the only person who
understands why you are doing what you're doing, walk
confidently along the path God paves for you.

Fellow leader, I'm challenging you to be a Christ-
follower who really does seek God's kingdom first. Be Jesus'

disciple in whatever arena you lead and conform yourself to his image in whatever situation you find yourself. Keep Christ first whenever the laws of leadership and the demands of discipleship collide.

# The Ministry of the Holy Spirit

Perhaps by now you're thinking: *But how do I know? I mean, when it gets right down to one of those collisions, how do I know what to do?*

The best response I can offer is simply a reminder that the ministry of the Holy Spirit is a very real, very accessible gift to be opened by every Christ-follower. John 16:13 promises that the Holy Spirit *always* will guide us down the best path, if only we will listen to his promptings. The Holy Spirit will give us God's mind on every matter when those collisions look inevitable. The longer I lead, the more dependent I become on his ministry and his whisper, not just for what I do at collision points but also—and especially—for day-by-day encouragement, guidance, and wisdom in all aspects of my life and my leadership.

Christian leaders cannot afford to wield influence apart from the direction of the Holy Spirit. It takes more than human-crafted leadership laws to be effective; the role of Scripture and of the ministry of the Holy Spirit can never be overestimated.

As I consider afresh how true it is that we as ministry leaders cannot operate apart from the Holy Spirit's work in our lives, I can't help but remember a time I probably would have imploded if it hadn't been for the Holy Spirit's intervention.

It takes more than human-crafted leadership laws to be effective; the role of Scripture and of the ministry of the Holy Spirit can never be overestimated.

During a tough ministry season, the general responsibilities of my role and some challenging extenuating circumstances were ganging up on me. Criticism was mounting, and I was in a pressure cooker to beat all pressure cookers. I knew if I didn't get away and spend some private time with God, I was going to blow. It wouldn't be a pretty sight.

I drove away from the Willow Creek campus, got on a boat, and took it out on Lake Michigan, as far as I could from any sight of land.

You should know that I don't make a habit of asking for signs and wonders from God, but on this particular day, that's exactly what I did. I needed a word, a signal, *some* indication from God that the seemingly devastating leadership complexities I faced wouldn't take me out of the game altogether. "God, please let me hear from you. I know I'm supposed to be more mature than this, but today, I'm not. I need some kind of reassurance here that I'm not in this alone. I can't keep leading the charge if I feel like I'm all alone."

I know this may sound mystical or maybe a little silly . . . or even presumptuous. But on my knees on the deck of a boat in the middle of a lake, it's precisely what I said to God.

And in response to my agonized request, there was silence. Perfect silence.

For a while, I wondered if God was otherwise occupied, but before my faith could falter, God gave me three thoughts. He conveyed them so forcefully and with such clarity that I ran below deck, grabbed a pencil and paper, and began to scribble them down so that I could remember them exactly as they were given.

Here was thought number one: *Bill, you are a treasured child of the most high God.*

That was the phrase, exactly as I received it: "You are a treasured child of the most high God." Every word in that phrase was a gift to me. Bill, *you*, with all your faults and sin and junk and with all the fear you have right now; *you are*—you are right now, not someday when you get to

> I sat and I read
> those words over and over
> again that day on that boat.
> And I cried. *I'm a treasured child
> of the most high God.*
> How could I have lost
> sight of that?

heaven, someday when you're stronger and you have your
act together better than you do today; you are right now a
*treasured child*—not an orphaned child, not a stepchild, not
even a mildly appreciated child. You are a treasured child
of the *most high God, the most high God,* through whom all
things are possible.

It was like God was saying: *Bill, remember who
you are. And remember whose you are.*

I sat and I read those words over and over again
that day on that boat. And I cried. *I'm a treasured child of
the most high God.* How could I have lost sight of that?

The second thought that came to me from the Spirit went like this: *The cause that I have assigned to you is going to prevail, and the combined forces of darkness cannot defeat it.*

What a powerful reminder! Somewhere along the way, I had forgotten the words of Jesus, who said, in essence, in Matthew 16:18, "I'm going to build my church, and the gates of hell won't prevail against it."

That revelation lifted a heavy, heavy burden off my shoulders. I thought: *Yes, I'm involved in a really tough battle right here, right now; but the church of Jesus Christ has survived two thousand years of battles, many of which raged a whole lot hotter than this one. God is going to make sure that his church survives and thrives until Christ's return. The ultimate responsibility for the victory of his church is on his shoulders, not mine.*

Then came the Spirit's final words that day: *I have surrounded you with some of the most loving, remarkable Christ-followers in the world. Lean into them. Let them love you. Invite them into your struggle. Ask for their help. Ask for their prayers.*

Within hours of getting back to the dock, I did just that.

The great leader T. D. Jakes once told me that when you have face-to-face issues, problems, or confrontations with others, it's all different when you've first been face-to-face with God. Although my experience on the boat that day may seem crazy, it enabled me to get face-to-face with God. And that made all the difference. My circumstances had not changed one bit, but by the time I got back to the dock that afternoon, my spirit had shifted, my heart had expanded, and my courage had regained its footing.

> When you have face-to-face issues, problems, or confrontations with others, it's all different when you've first been face-to-face with God.

My point? Just a simple reminder that the power of the Holy Spirit is the leader's best friend. The one who stands alongside you when leadership gets lonely . . . that's the Holy Spirit. The one who guides and gives you strength when leadership gets confusing . . . that's the Holy Spirit. The one who warns you of pitfalls and whispers words of renewal when you grow weary . . . that's the Holy Spirit. The one who reminds you that you are a treasured child of the most high God . . . *that's* the Holy Spirit.

Maybe the Holy Spirit wants to remind you right now, in your role as a leader, that the cause God has

If you know the laws of leadership and follow them when they should be followed, if you love God and readily follow the prompting of his Spirit when you sense he is guiding, then you will make it.

assigned to you is indeed going to prevail. God's kingdom will be built. His name will be glorified. But it's not all on your shoulders. Christ has secured the victory.

Or maybe you are going through a high-stakes challenge and you've never opened up your heart to the people around you to tell them how hard your challenge is. Friend, if God has surrounded you with remarkable, loving people, then lean into them. Try facing the challenge as a team instead of alone, as an individual. Maybe you need to show the kind of vulnerability Jesus showed in the Garden of Gethsemane when he said, essentially, "You know what? This is hard. It's *really* hard."

If you know the laws of leadership and follow them when they should be followed, if you love God and readily follow the prompting of his Spirit when you sense he is guiding, then you will make it. And when there's a collision, if you say, "I'm going to decide on the side of discipleship and the clear teachings of Scripture every time. I'm going to put my hand in the Holy Spirit's hand all day,

every day, and allow him to be my guide and my strength,"
then you will make it.

In fact, you won't just "make it"—you will thrive.
You won't just thrive—you will *prevail*! And you will be able
to overcome whatever the forces of darkness throw at you,
guaranteed.

# Fighting Words

The proof of that guarantee is in one little verse,
found in the book of Nehemiah.

Nehemiah and the people had been working
day and night to rebuild the broken-down wall around
Jerusalem, and right in the middle of their backbreaking
efforts, enemies sent word that they were going to come in
with troops and massacre the whole lot of them.

Understandably, the people were more than a
little jittery.

Knowing he had to make some sort of leadership
move, Nehemiah gathered everyone together and gave

them a challenge. In essence, Nehemiah 4:14 says, "Remember God, who is great and awesome, and then fight with all your might."

I love those words! *Remember God*—he is for you. He loves you. He is more than just enough. You are a treasured child of the most high God. And then, *fight with all your might*—give the cause of Christ your all!

As you face your daily responsibilities as a leader, this is my simple charge from Nehemiah straight to you: Remember God, who is great and awesome. Remember God, who is faithful and true. Remember God, who is ever-present in times of turmoil. Remember God, who has promised to pull you through.

And then the second part: Fight with all your might. Fight for the lives and hearts of people far from God. Fight to recruit volunteers. Fight for resources for the poor and the forgotten. Fight to build a business that serves with integrity and distinction. Fight to save God's creation and to bring peace and justice to earth. Fight to build schools and communities and organizations that reflect God's kingdom. Fight *with all your might* for your church to become a full-blown Acts 2 expression in your community.

Whatever your leadership endeavor, give God all of the glory. And one day we'll all meet in heaven, where we can celebrate his goodness forever.

## LEADERSHIP DEVELOPMENT MATTERS

The Leadership Summit, a two-and-a-half day event, convenes every August in the Chicago area and is satellite broadcast live to more than 130 locations across North America. Designed for leaders in any arena—ministry, business, nonprofit—its purpose is to encourage and equip Christian leaders with an injection of vision, skill development, and inspiration.

**For up-to-date information about The Leadership Summit, visit www.willowcreek.com/summit**

# Making Vision Stick

Andy Stanley

Vision is the lifeblood of your organization.

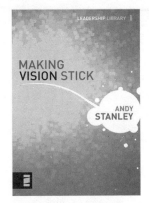

It should be coursing through the minds and hearts of those you lead, focusing their creativity and galvanizing their efforts. Together, you and your team will strive to make your vision a reality.

But in order for that to happen, you've got to make your vision stick. That's your responsibility as the leader.

Pastor and author Andy Stanley first shows you the reasons why vision doesn't stick. Then, sharing vivid firsthand examples, he walks you through five simple but powerful ways to make your vision infiltrate the hearts, minds, and lives of those you lead.

*Making Vision Stick* provides the keys you need to propel your organization forward.

Hardcover: 0-310-28305-1

*Pick up a copy today at your favorite bookstore!*

# Holy Discontent
## Fueling the Fire that Ignites Personal Vision

Bill Hybels

What is the one aspect of this broken world that is so troubling it gets you off the couch and moves you to take action? This is what Bill Hybels refers to as a holy discontent: a personal "firestorm of frustration" that can catalyze fierce determination to set things right. It is often during these eye-opening moments that you hear God whisper, "I feel the exact same way about this situation. Now, let's go solve it together!"

Hybels invites you to consider the dramatic impact your life will have when you willingly convert the frustration of your holy discontent into fuel for changing the world.

Hardcover: 0-310-27228-9
Audio CD: 0-310-27735-3

*Pick up a copy today at your favorite bookstore!*

www.willowcreek.com

# Living and Leading from Your Holy Discontent
## A Companion Guide for Ministry Leaders

Bill Hybels with Ashley Wiersma

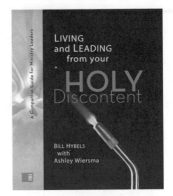

In this companion workbook to *Holy Discontent*, Bill Hybels helps you to discover your own holy discontent, and then shows you how to use it as a never-ending fuel source for your ministry.

You'll learn how to uncover the holy discontent not only in yourself, but also in the lives of those you lead. Then you can identify and feed the collective holy discontent of your church or organization, so that together you can tackle some of the toughest problems around you. The result? An energized, purposeful ministry that taps into the passions of its people to change the world for Christ.

Softcover: 0-310-28290-X

*Pick up a copy today at your favorite bookstore!*

www.willowcreek.com

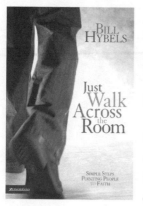

# Just Walk Across the Room
## A Four-Week Church Experience

Bill Hybels

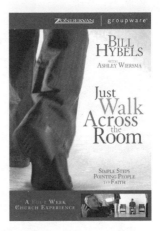

Join thousands of churches nationwide in launching the complete four-week campaign experience based on the book, *Just Walk Across the Room*.

The kit provides everything your church needs for four weeks of Sunday services and midweek small group discussions, including:

- CD-ROM
- Small Group DVD with Leader's Guide
- Participant's Guide
- *Just Walk Across the Room* Hardcover Book
- Quick-Start Guide

Kit: 0-310-27172-X
Participant's Guide: 0-310-27176-2
Small Group DVD: 0-310-27174-6

*Pick up a copy today at your favorite bookstore!*

# Courageous Leadership

Bill Hybels

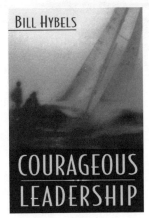

Are you a 360-degree leader? Three-hundred-sixty-degree leaders don't just direct their gift of leadership south, to the people under their care. They also learn to lead north by influencing those with authority over them, and to lead east and west by impacting their peers. But most importantly, they learn how to keep the compass needle centered by leading themselves—by keeping their own lives in tune so they can provide maximum direction for others.

Bill Hybels shares lessons he has learned about the gift of spiritual leadership and its strategic importance within the church. Based on the thirty years he has led Willow Creek Community Church, this book is a must-read for all church leaders and their teams.

Hardcover: 0-310-24823-X

*Pick up a copy today at your favorite bookstore!*

www.willowcreek.com

This resource was created to serve you and to help you build a local church that prevails. It is just one of many ministry tools that are part of the Willow Creek Resources® line, published by the Willow Creek Association together with Zondervan.

The Willow Creek Association (WCA) was created in 1992 to serve a rapidly growing number of churches from across the denominational spectrum that are committed to helping unchurched people become fully-devoted followers of Christ. Membership in the WCA now numbers over 12,000 Member Churches worldwide from more than ninety denominations.

The Willow Creek Association links like-minded Christian leaders with each other and with strategic vision, training and resources in order to help them build prevailing churches designed to reach their redemptive potential. Here are some of the ways the WCA does that.

**The Leadership Summit**—A once a year, two-and-a-half-day learning experience to envision and equip Christians with leadership gifts and responsibilities. Presented live on Willow's campus as well as via satellite simulcast to over 135 locations across North America—plus more than eighty international cities feature the Summit by way of videocast every Fall—this event is designed to increase the leadership effectiveness of pastors, ministry staff, volunteer church leaders and Christians in the marketplace.

**Ministry-Specific Conferences**—Throughout the year the WCA hosts a variety of conferences and training events—both at Willow Creek's main campus and offsite, across North America and around the world. These events are for church leaders and volunteers in areas such as group life, children's ministry, student ministry, preaching and teaching, the arts and stewardship.

 **Willow Creek Resources®**—Provides churches with trusted and field-tested ministry resources on important topics such as leadership, volunteer ministries, spiritual formation, stewardship, evangelism, group life, children's ministry, student ministry, the arts and more.

 **WCA Member Benefits**—Includes substantial discounts to WCA training events, a 20 percent discount on all Willow Creek Resources®, *Defining Moments* monthly audio journal for leaders, quarterly *Willow* magazine, access to a Members-Only section on WCA's web site, monthly communications and more. Member Churches also receive special discounts and premier services through the WCA's growing number of ministry partners—Select Service Providers—and save an average of $500 annually depending on the level of engagement.

**For specific information about WCA conferences, resources, membership, and other ministry services, contact:**

Willow Creek Association
P.O. Box 3188, Barrington, IL 60011-3188
Phone: 847-570-9812 • Fax: 847-765-5046
www.willowcreek.com

We want to hear from you.

Please send your comments about this book

to us in care of zreview@zondervan.com. Thank you.